Meta Verse

Meta Verse

A Collection of Lyrical Reflections

by
MARK E. QUIRK

RESOURCE *Publications* • Eugene, Oregon

META VERSE
A Collection of Lyrical Reflections

Resource Publications
An Imprint of Wipf and Stock Publishers
199 W. 8th Ave., Suite 3
Eugene, OR 97401

www.wipfandstock.com

PAPERBACK ISBN: 979-8-3852-0921-7
HARDCOVER ISBN: 979-8-3852-0922-4
EBOOK ISBN: 979-8-3852-0923-1

04/23/24

To Janice, for whom I've been writing poetry since we were sweethearts in high school.

CONTENTS

PREFACE

OH, HOW I'VE YEARNED to reach out to you through poetry! When I was 12 years old, I published my first poetry collection in a magazine called the Bantam Gazette (yes, chickens). It was self- published, and each copy was handwritten by me and a friend. At five cents per issue, it sold quite well during its short, labor-intensive existence. When word spread to the teachers' lounge that we were collecting money, we ended up in the principal's office. Turns out that student entrepreneurship was unacceptable in our middle school at the time. If anyone still possesses a copy, I would love to talk with you.

Many years have passed since those first poems were published. Along the way I've produced a small number of poems for family and friends to feed my passion and most importantly to communicate emotion, thoughts, and reflections at special events in a manner that no other written or oral medium would convey. During those five decades I've also authored academic books about the importance of using reflective thinking and effective communication to enhance our lives and our relationships.

This is my chance to put the two together and offer you an opportunity through poetry to think about your own thoughts, emotions, and values as they relate to many of the important themes of our times. It's also an opportunity for us to explore, renew, and act upon our values to protect them in a sometimes-chaotic world. The rhythmic couplets, quatrains, and sexains herein provide the background harmony for our contemplative adventure. Please enjoy reading this collection of poems in *Meta Verse* as much as I've enjoyed writing it.

THIS MOMENT

What we crave our words but cry.
Tomorrow's gift today is shy.
We burst with hope forever more,
Relying on our lives before
For meaning that reflections give.
Time now for love and life to live.

No regrets as time moves on,
Each moment savored in a song.
Tomorrow brings another star —
A constellation from afar,
Together looking all the same:
A picture clearer than each frame.

Majestic mountains past the shoal
Where waves march twice and lovers stroll.
Warm sunshine feeds all shades of blue,
A glistening gem this dream come true.
The tides of time, the lows, the highs,
Tomorrow brings a new sunrise.

Like the tree that marks the spot
Where stories shared and mangos bought.
Limbs heavy, stretching to the clouds,
With leaves that dance and sing aloud.
Today's events will come and go,
The memories left we hold to show.

Look around with open eyes.
Breathe deep and touch the sun-filled skies.
The beauty that surrounds and bathes
Our soul, so distant through the haze,

Walks out of shadows in disguise,
If only we do recognize.

To recollect and reaffirm
Our course laid out with every turn.
The here and now we set aside
To chase tomorrow's dreams that hide.
For better times we choose to long,
But in this moment, we belong.

HORN OF PLENTY

Fields of wheat, rice, cane, and corn:
A horn of plenty for babies born.
Peach, pear, and apple trees:
Eat as much as you would please.
Cans and boxes pack the aisles:
Markets burst with piles and piles.

A child looks up with sunken face,
Skin-draped bones, eyes froze in place.
He screams in silence, questions why.
No tears for fear death passes by.
Food we burn that would go bad,
So far away if only had.

Great men and women fill the halls,
Our students smartest of them all.
Gold and silver chase we might,
While those who suffer out of sight
Remind us who we really are,
No mirrors show this ugly scar.

Surrender greed to love life now.
Divide our wealth and share the plough
With those of us who need it most.
No children dying as we boast
Of greatness made turned upside down
In cities viewed from each small town.

The voicemail box so long was filled
With messages of children killed.
Tomorrow came the last day's dawn.
We failed to act for those who mourn.

Our time was spent creating things
That sunlight-blinded meaning brings.

SPACE TRAVEL

What's it like to travel back
In time? To go between the crack
That marks the spot to be exact,
When yesterday became tomorrow:
The point where time from both was borrowed —
Today's regrets can't turn to sorrow.

It's the same to travel space,
Where time it takes becomes a race
To find the speck you call your place.
From here to there the time between
Can't be felt or touched or seen.
So, in its place becomes a dream.

Our time in space we age with grace.
The wrinkles on our hands and face
Don't have a reason to take place
Without the minutes or the hours
That define those other powers
Who take control of time not ours.

We chase the dream to fly up there,
Above the birds, the sky, thin air.
To the crack that space will share
With time that stops yet never starts.
We yearn to spread our wings apart,
To welcome all the healing hearts.

TAPESTRY

Life is like a tapestry,
Hand-made, its core a mystery.
The hidden warp provides its strength,
A weft-faced weave the fabric's length.
Artistic beauty side we see,
Belies the tension underneath.

We use the loom to weave the weft,
Our actions driven right and left.
Not guided by our values clear,
The warp so hidden failed to steer
Toward lives of others more in need,
No homes to live with mouths to feed.

Expose the warp and tighten thread.
Save life's tree before it's dead.
What lies ahead our finest hours,
Not me or mine but all of ours.
A common purpose number one,
The decency to get things done.

EARTH'S BLACK BOX

From down under peer inside,
A world no secrets left to hide.
Come with me and take a look,
The story now an open book.
As bright light faded and gave way to black,
We turned upside down — came off the track.

Amazing beauty, innocence prevailed.
The earth's demise because we failed.
Without a clue we sowed the seed,
Then brash irreverence blurred the need
To halt the madness, change the course,
While few among us showed remorse.

Through avarice and greed, we showed
How meaningless can be life's road.
When self it seems to matter most,
We've nothing left that we could boast.
It's humankind that we lost touch,
What mattered most did not that much.

With sadness and with great regret
I tell you that the stage was set
For all to watch what we had built
Turn back to dust and rock and silt.
And then they came to help us see
Through smog filled skies what we could be.

The greatest story ever told
Relies upon the young, not old.
For years we sat upon a stage
Where wisdom failed to grow with age.

Then they were here to help us see
That life for all meant more than me.

At first their presence barely felt.
When they crawled, we stooped and knelt
To coax them on to take first steps.
Their wisdom grew beyond our depths,
Releasing us from who we were,
Our love for them and their future.

TWILIGHT

In between the moon and sun
A glow that lights the rabbit's run.
Time to muse and slow the pace,
A stroll more fun than is the race.

Reconnect the parts that matter,
Tame the urge to climb the ladder.
Define yourself by who you are.
What you've become has come so far.

Tomorrow's chores can always wait
Till yesterday's are off your plate.
Was first, now last and not so fast,
To see so clear no shadows cast.

The sun will set and that we know.
As night appears the embers glow.
The story that's today will end
With twilight messages that we send.

Hearts around us that we touch,
Especially those we love so much,
Are there with us to set the stage,
As we prepare for life's last page.

DANCER

She loves to dance and sway her hips.
Silver locks, silk skin, and ruby lips.
Timeless beauty, God's good grace,
Seductive smile ignites her face.
A youthful frame belies her age,
More a story than a page.

At center stage a wonderous heart.
Her dance is brilliant, not just smart.
She gives once more and then again.
We watch amazed, a perfect ten.
Each pirouette becomes a stare,
Imagine twirling body bare.

The day will fill with work and chore,
Impatient wait to dance once more.
As dusk sets in, the floor is clear,
Hearts race ahead as time gets near.
She beckons you to join the fun,
A steamy vortex spinning one.

The night moves drift from dance to dreams
With love made blurred by in between.
Morning haze a dreamy blue,
A distant shadow swirls anew.
She will dance through time forever,
Lasting gift that just gets better.

CAROUSEL

They stare at me; I want to hide.
Their legs fly high with every stride.
With manes that flow and teeth so bare,
They're beautiful and yet I'm scared.
Today I'll do it, show you all,
Hang on for life so not to fall.

My heart is thumping, clench my teeth,
A long way up from underneath.
Those hoofs so real with golden shoes.
My saddle's wide, no reigns to use.
I promise you that I won't cry
If you this once stand by my side.

Oh, here we go, no turning back.
Hold tight he shouts, my fingers crack.
I'm flying now and feeling fine.
A chill that tingles up my spine.
I can't stop smiling, feeling bold,
Invincible at four years old.

GREAT ESCAPE

Today's first breath so fresh and clean.
The scent that lingers evergreen.
Crickets' a cappella bold,
Life's cradle sways to calm the old.
A spider swings on her trapeze,
The sights and sounds so sure to please.

Subtleties of life's great pleasure,
So routine and hard to measure.
We sometimes leave our soul behind,
And when we search it's hard to find.
We breathe so deep to quench our thirst,
We often fail to see life first.

Daylight turns from bright to dim,
Tomorrow's dawn the air is thin.
Wind-swept rains avoid the plains,
Instead wreak havoc causing pain
To those who work so hard and toil,
Tending stock and turning soil.

As smoke-filled hills reach toward the sea,
The time is now for you and me
To be the heroes in those eyes
That see right through us when we die.
Gains we've made to better lives,
Set back by motives so contrived.

Take in the sights and sounds outdoors,
As birds rejoice, now give them more
Hope to live the life they know,
As Mother Nature planned it so.

The need for change is crystal clear.
It's time to act; the exodus near.

DIVIDED

Knees bent down on straining neck.
One man's life gains no respect.
A picture blazoned in our mind,
Like branding iron, humankind.

History repeats itself.
Again, our sordid past is felt.
Tomorrow brings another day.
Who's the next in line to pay?

To break the cycle, see it clear.
Give up the power, conquer fear.
Injustice sets a lowly bar.
Self-righteousness can't hide the scar.

Heal the wounds that we inflict
On those our fathers did depict
As tools of trade and mouths to feed,
A country set on course by greed.

We can change; it's not too late.
Reach out with love, denounce the hate.
Accept how different people are,
Much like the heavens with each star.

ARTIFICIAL INTELLIGENCE

Hi Siri. How should I feel?
There's a war going on in a faraway place.
I'm not sure if it's fake or if it's real.
It doesn't exist in my time or space.

On TV I see some people
Who shoot at others that die where they lay.
Just to the left is a brilliant steeple,
Mourners in pews sob as they pray.

Siri, I could sure use your advice.
My husband has cancer and might lose his jobs.
What can I do and what is the price
To stay strong and smile as my heart twists and throbs?

My kids go to school, and I'm gone when they're home.
I finish my shift and head back at night.
I see them on weekends when they're not on their phone.
They say that they love me; do you think that they might?

Maybe ChatGPT can clear up my head,
Give me some hope for a happier life,
Put food on my table and lessen my dread,
Make me a better mom and a caring wife.

DARE TO HOPE

I feared my maker had abandoned me
For eating from the forbidden tree,
Persevering when the times were worst,
When all felt lost, dark clouds that burst.
By hope eternal made my way
To times shined brighter day by day.

When skies, that looked so bad at first,
Released the rain to feed my thirst
And helped the tree of life to grow,
That gave me shade for love to sow.
Each time my heart would sink so much,
New hope would come with light to touch.

Take my hand and hold it tight,
For all to see and in plain sight.
Together we will make it through
And share the joy inside of you.
Enough to overcome the pain,
A newfound hope that's not in vain.

To forge a future where the sun is bright,
And daytime bridges dreams from night.
Tomorrow brings new love to share
With others. That is why we dare
to clearly see with open eyes
The good that comes with each sunrise.

COMMUNICATION

Don't tell my phone when what you need
Is more than just to speak at me.
Face to face and eye to eye,
Tell it straight; don't try to hide
Behind a message or a text
For fear of what will happen next.

It only takes a minute more
To walk the hall, knock on the door.
I'll greet you with a happy smile,
And thank you for the extra mile.
Now close your eyes to really see
Who we are, both you and me.

Hear my breath from deep inside;
That inner space, nowhere to hide.
It's from the heart you find that word
To say to me you think absurd.
What matters most is what you feel.
That moment said is time for real.

ELEVATOR TALK

M: "Good morning, could you push two please?"

Y: "Sure." *You're closer. Why ask me?*

M: "Weather's great – a clear blue sky!"

Y: "Yeh." *It's still cold, why even try!*

M: "The beds are great, best sleep yet."

Y: Stare. *The blanket was thick – I woke up in a sweat.*

M: "Cup of coffee, then flying home today!"

Y: "Safe travels." *If I don't close this deal, there'll be hell to pay.*

GIANT REDWOODS

To walk among these giant trees
My soul released, my spirit freed.
I'm home again the trip so long,
My roots exposed where I belong.
I feel the quiet strength within
To persevere through thick and thin.

The family grove is tightly knit.
For centuries side by side they sit
Until the time that one must leave,
To start anew with his own seed.
Again, to reach the greatest height
Among his own and packed so tight.

.

They stand up high, all dressed in red.
Their weaker peers are long since dead,
Succumbed to flames and wind no match
For these great giants standing watch.
Above the clouds their tops protrude,
Bathed in fog to set the mood.

The tree of life a story told
Of family time with young and old.
Together finding greater strength
Through love, life's value meant
To live so long and grow so tall
For generations, thriving all.

OIL SPILL

Black licorice feathers try to fly
On wings that reach up toward the sky.
Grey tears rain down on fish that drown,
Pure white sand now dirty brown.
Once pristine our sea and shore,
A fading memory nothing more.

Gigantic beasts that rust and weep.
From gaping holes their cargo seeps.
Goo fills the gills of those who breathe
Through once pure water where conceived.
The vast oasis they call home,
Destroyed by selfish greed alone.

We see tomorrow's brighter skies
Through clearer windows free from lies.
We tell ourselves the other story,
Of our greatness in all its glory.
For going faster, reaching higher,
Chastising those for screaming fire!

Set aside our failed reaction.
Find a greater satisfaction
Knowing that our values true
Restore our seas to shades of blue
So that our daughter and your son
Can revel in the ocean's fun.

FLIGHT OF THE OSPREY

The king of raptors sounds so shrill
While flying over, flaunting kill.
The fish who suffer their demise
Are clueless reading his disguise.
As he appears out of the sky,
His razor hooks no chance to pry.

He soars above from shore to shore,
His talons filled with food for four.
Chicks that sit in patient wait
Till dad returns with fisher's bait.
He flashes catch to gulls with pride,
As great blue herons turn to hide.

The nest sits high above the grass,
A perch to measure those who pass.
This fearless warrior keeps an eye
For feckless transients who might try
To squat the site she marks as hers,
A move so bold, her stare deters.

We can learn from birds of prey,
When to hunt and when to stay.
The fittest of us all survive,
Believing in our catch we dive
In unknown waters day and night,
Steadfast our faith to guide the flight.

WOOLLY MAMMOTH

They're coming home a feat arranged,
Ten thousand years how things have changed.
They lived in times when we weren't born.
To see us now will make them mourn.

A million years when ice appeared,
These woolly creatures first were reared.
As cool warmed up and humans thrived,
We took it all, their kind deprived.

Now twenty years after Dolly,
Science will repeat the folly.
Bringing creatures back to life
To serve our purpose causing strife,
Repeating all the damage done
Not by climate or the sun.

CLARK'S ISLAND TRILOGY:
The Landing

The shallop roiled through sleet and gale,
With master's mate in charge of sail.
Eighteen men with clothes that froze,
Their bodies shaking head to toes.

The rudder snapped, no longer steered,
Through seas so great that all would fear.
The mast gave way and split in two.
They gave to God all they could do.

The waves did smash on rocks to pound.
A miracle to land on sandy ground.
Between the breach it made the beach
Inside the cove where storms won't reach.

Master Clark, his weary crew,
Tramped through the darkness fearing new.
Up the hill through brush and vines,
Sparked by hope of better times.

Through blinding snow a form appeared,
Placed well ahead a million years
To offer those who needed most
A sign of hope this rock did boast.

To wake right there near her side
Next morning Sabbath to preside.
A chance to rest this place does bring,
To choose to stay, give thanks and sing.

CLARK'S ISLAND TRILOGY:
Hop House

She stands aside her older brother,
Four score plus forty from t'other.

In the field of hops so plenty
she sits so proud, to please so many.

Warm sunshine and the beach surround,
A symphony without the sound.

Red tugboat chugs the channel toward
The bay beyond where boats are moored.

Shades of blue with green life's hue,
White framed glass for looking through.

Her modest presence shimmers souls
As angels' songs drown death knell tolls.

A lesson learned for all her peers,
That beauty comes from many years

That tally days and through the nights
Where strangers gather out of sight

Separated by their years alive
But joined together by their drive

To honor those who came before
And for those next through open door.

The bridge we are for those we make
Finds meaning in a funeral wake.

CLARK'S ISLAND TRILOGY:
T'Other House

The summer kitchen and borning room
Bely its age and greet the moon.
Pot belly stove that warms the heart
For those of us so far apart.

The kitchen well, its hatch secure,
Our drinking water clear and pure.
The secrets shared by those who eat
Will stay forever in each seat.

A hanging lamp that's filled with oil
Gives light enough for clams to boil.
The rain pours down to soak the soil,
Bearing fruit for those who toil
And till the earth from turnip seeds.
We give God thanks when fall concedes.

Fine stoneware from the Dutch,
with windmills turning in the hutch.
Delft tiles circle winter's fire,
Warming souls of those who tire.

Cupboard doors built into brick
Tell stories of the scared and sick.
Harrowing days and nights in storm
Pushed families round the fire to warm.
Their courage stretched beyond their time,
The will to live for next in line.

Tall shadows in the field surround
Trees standing guard, not making sounds.
Black walnut stretches far and wide,
Beyond stone walls and toward the tide.
Giant lindens reach for the sky,
While stalwart cedars question why.

Their scent reminds us of the day
When fancy chests were made to stay,
Forever holding skirts of silk,
Free from moths and nests they built.
Green feathers swaying in the breeze,
Since pilgrim days they live to please.

Beyond the walnut tree that thrives,
A giant barn its walls survived,
To tell of whaling boats it built
And store the ploughs for soil they tilled.
This place alive with memories
Is shared by all as history.

FALL GARDEN

Like lumpy oatmeal, summer's soil rests under a warm blanket of
withered seaweed.

The brilliant noontime sun soothes your nose in the crisp fall air
and bares the shadows at your feet.

Patiently lying rusted rake and hoe guard the wooden gate,
beside the empty pails turned upside down to sleep.

Two weathered oyster shells peer from beneath the leafless
honeysuckle bush, weary of the spiders spinning webs.

The tangle of fruitless grapevines, now knotted twine,
are all the fence these sacred grounds require.

The smooth-skinned silver birch waves good-bye as swallows
dance up in the sky.

ORCHARD

Fall is here with cooling nights.
Bright colored leaves bring maple bites.
The time to stroll among the trees
And fill your bag with Macs that please.

We'll make our dumplings, crisps, and pies.
Eat them fresh while crust doughs rise.
With fruit that's left when all is done
We'll make as sauce with cinnamon.

And don't forget the cider too.
It warms the cockles through and through.
As summer breeze brings calming chills,
We shift from ocean to the hills.

In fall we love the fruits of life.
We see ourselves sweet as the night.
Then winter comes before we sleep
To store the memories that we keep.

COUNTRY FAIR

Crisp fall air makes fog at sea,
The dew in valleys clings to trees.
The weather's right for picking pears
And traveling to our country fairs.
The journey comes but once a year,
A pilgrimage the faithful cheer.

We pack the van with kids and snacks.
By dinner time we'll all be back.
Excitement grows as we come closer,
Shown on billboards, giant posters.
Pictures of the Ferris wheel,
Joyful riders, disk of steel.

As we arrive, walk through the gate,
It brings back memories of this date,
When giant cups and worms that fly
Right by our heads on either side.
Next to sheep, dogs testing skills,
While baby goats send us warm chills.

The time flew by, hard to believe,
It's after five and time to leave.
The kids are tired and walking slow,
And soon they'll fall asleep we know.
While dreaming of the day that's done
Their lives are richer, full of fun.

RENEWAL

The first time we saw our life together,
We saw a flower that grew in any weather.
We walked the aisle and exchanged our vow.
Remember then, forever is here and now.

Our time to celebrate and reaffirm with joy,
The miracle that bore a princess and curious boy.
The life we lived from then to now
Brought pure happiness as life allowed.

Now's the time to recollect what reaffirms
Our love that brought us through twists and turns,
As seasons changed and winds of time blew,
All signs that old had changed to new.

The time to live our life together
Is now and not to think forever.
Every minute, every hour
Should not be yours or mine but our.

NEW PARENTS

Shades of grey at dawn's first light,
Signs of life, a birds first flight.
Alive again with sounds and smells,
The new day born since wedding bells.

Live to love your life ahead.
A newborn's cry heard from your bed.
Through open door young whispers heard,
Tomorrow's dreams unspoken words.

Stay strong and fit, no time to sit.
So much to do for them and you.
And through it all, it's two not one,
To share the tears and all the fun.

Together you're most happy when
You do those simple things, and then,
Take some time to share the joy
That life's distractions can't destroy.

Today will mark that point in time
When things are ours, no longer mine.
And as each year begins anew
The dreams you share will all come true.

FAMILY TREE

Our life together is in front of us. We can live here a couple of
years.
Cinder block shower. Food stamps. No fears. We know how to
cut back.
We chase our dreams.
That's who we are.

"You can push now," she says gently. "But where's the doctor?"
"He should be here any minute. I can see the head." I'm feeling
dread.
I can see three of them down the line.
Straining then resting, crying in pain and then with joy.
Oh my, it's a boy!

So how do we figure this out? Make it work? Pay the rent? Not
what I meant.
Let's move to the country. Somewhere off the beaten path. Chop
wood for heat.
Warm our feet. Near a river. Covered bridge.
Make winding track through trees to sled. We love the outdoors.
Build a fire. Make s'mores.
That's who we are.

So how do we figure this out? Find better schools? Pay the bills?
Buy our pills?
But it's Christmas weekend! Our hearts are set on a mountaintop.
A gentleman's farm. Not quite. The five of us can sleep on the
floor while we fix it up.
And do dishes in the tub. Teaberries on the path. Our own
pond. We can bond.
I picture it. Make it happen.
That's who we are.

I know what I'm doing. Leave me alone. I can take care of
myself.
Give them just enough rope to not hang themselves. To learn.
Not burn.
Stay safe.
They become caring, independent, wonderful human beings.
That's who they are.

So how do we figure this out? Help them pay the rent? Make a
dent.
"You can push now." I can see the head. Can we do it all over
again?
They are so tiny. The love they share with those stares warms us
with a smile. Our lives enriched. The memories. We've turned
the corner together. The focus shifting.
Life's too short.

THROUGH THE YEARS

Sixteen now and all grown up.
You know it all, no more a pup.
Please read the signs that keep you safe.
Our sleepless nights, your great escape.

Celebrate at twenty-eight, you're looking great.
Sharp mind to match your hasty gait.
Tomorrow's here, another year,
No questions asked, no past to fear.

At thirty-six you're feeling fine, don't have a dime.
The family takes up most your time.
Costs are high, debt to the sky,
Forever 'ours' replaces 'my.'

It's half your life, statistics say,
But forty-five feels young, let's play.
Your life's ok and right on track.
The course you took no turning back.

Now sixty-nine you made it through, the two of you.
Your kids, they look like you, and act it too.
Though times were tough, you needed stuff.
You had each other, just enough.

Eighty-five with hope alive.
Two steps forward, even stride.
Sunset now, the tide retreats.
Mistakes were made with few repeats.

It's time to go, to say good-bye.
Life's great escape, all set to die.

It's been a dream from there to here,
With no regrets nor much to fear.

MOM

Reach out and take my hand.
My first cry, first step, my first fall.
Cradle me as I learn to stand.
Your strength, my gift through it all.

Your light's my beacon through the night.
An island safe from all my fears.
You wrap your arms around me tight,
And share with me your love and tears.

Letting go, to say good-bye,
A leap of faith will be my guide
To answer all the questions why,
What lies ahead on the other side.

I'll hold your hand till your last breath,
When your eyes will close to see so clear
The past that is our future after death,
Forever held in time to keep you near.

DAD

Hey there, how's it going?
Okay I guess (. . . not really knowing).
You recognize me deep inside.
Those vacant eyes the truth can't hide.
I've seen that face . . . maybe . . . it's been a while.
I'm not sure. Can't place that smile.

How's your roommate Drew?
He's good, I think. Not sure. Who?
How've the meals been, good?
That look, not sure he understood.
I'm hungry; is it time to eat?
Not yet, let's talk; I'll have a seat.

Mom is sick, they say it's bad.
Okay.   I'm sorry that's so sad.
Fine boy, she must be very nice.
That stare, those eyes, as cold as ice.
I know it's him and yet it's not.
Are memories more real than thought?

A tear or sweat, it's really hot.
I just don't know what is or not.
Good talking, Dad. I'll see you soon.
Nice young man. It must be noon.
Can't wait to eat. It's time to go.
Though he's not the same, I love him so.

CENTENARIAN

Life so full with those you love,
And then the call from up above.
It's time to go, for now at least.
Your Spirit thrives, your life deceased.

Each person touched becomes a light
To shine on others in their sight.
Imprinted with your special sign,
A soul that stands the test of time.

With those you shared a life well-meant,
Who thrived upon the love you sent,
Expand the circle inside out,
So all can share and leave no doubt.

Your virtues praised by those you met.
The care you showed so blatant yet,
Expecting nothing in return to get.
And now it's time for your sunset.

Going forward what would you expect
Us to do, and be, as we reflect
Upon your life so full of worth,
A hundred years to death from birth.

To be yourself and love each day.
Move with purpose, don't just say
You'll do your best but plant the seed.
Show you care for all who need.

FRIEND

Hey, you got a minute?
Shoot the breeze, converse a bit?

Sixty seconds of your time?
Too much to ask at a drop of a dime?

What do you say about forever?
That's the time we could be together.

I'd like to get to know you, please.
Life's too short and talk's a breeze.

KNOCK, KNOCK! WHO'S THERE?

Your next door neighbor.
Can I come in?
Tell me first the color of your skin.
It's kind of brown, perhaps it's tan.
I don't have money, but I have a plan.

Oh. I don't know, did you fill out forms?
Can you read English, follow the norms?
Agree to quietly make their beds,
Take out the trash and cut those dreads?

I crossed the river, not too deep.
My kids in tow didn't sleep.
Spent the past ten years in terror,
Looking for something a whole lot better.

I saw your passage on TV.
Looked like a rodeo to me.
Those horses, they were really scared,
The way they reared with teeth so bared.

I think you need to wait to enter,
Stay in that detention center.
Then go back, get yourself together.
We'll let you know when things get better.

THE TRANSCENDENTALIST

My God for me I know him best.
My right to join or not attest.

My nature is to be my own.
My God is mine and mine alone.

My intuition oversees.
My only truth it comes from me.

My questions and their answers be.
My nature wild and fancy free.

The easy way is not to care,
To look away, avoid despair.

The higher road for all to take,
Create the good for goodness' sake.

It's in our nature to do well,
Despite the few who would dispel.

This truth we know and cannot hide.
We're one with nature by our side.

It's time to live the simple life,
Avoid excess with all its strife.

Touch the soil around the roots,
Such dirty hands that can't pollute.

Your mind will feed the empty soul,
The lavish life that took its toll.

LUCK

Sprawled in my reclining chair,
Watching all the ads that air.
Now it's time for Lottery Live.
Aspiring actress weekly strives
To liven up the boring spot
Where dreams are made or go to pot.

No single viewer could care less
About her clothes or hair, a mess.
Subconsciously, I reach my hand,
Back pocket, wallet, ticket, stand
To get it out and read along,
Join the TV viewing throng.

Never won a thing before,
Perhaps a ticket nothing more.
Just to feed my gambling need,
I bet I'll lose although I'll plead.
The ping pong balls pop like corn.
First ball's a winner, dream is born.

The second ball, a lucky 7.
I feel I've died and gone to heaven.
My birthday's next what're the chances?
To win four hundred it slowly dances
Into the slot, it's 31,
A baby's born, a healthy son!

The fourth ball from the spinning drum,
A 6, my God, I'm feeling numb!
Mom-in-law is next in line.
Her day for me is here to shine.

Yikes 21, I'm feeling hazy,
I swear I'll never call her crazy.

The next ball seems to take forever.
Time stands still, she pulls the lever.
Like a feather it floats in air.
This moment makes it seem unfair.
My heart jumps through my chest.
I hold my breath, here comes the test.

Our anniversary, it's 23, at last!!
Euphoria sets in and all the past
Seems so clear our life to live,
How much to save, how much to give.
For now, I'll savor how I feel.
It's all I have, what's left of real.

THE REAL YOU

Close your eyes to really see
What your life can truly be.

Plug your ears to block the noise
That interferes with sounds of joy.

Smells of spring are in the air,
A time to share with those we care.

Touch my hand to let me know
How much it is you love me so.

WRITER'S BLOCK

The wall so clear but not a word.
You listen but you haven't heard.

They're in there somewhere, hard to find,
Like black on black or never mind.

Be patient, let your thoughts roam free.
Close your eyes so you may see

What lurks behind those big, closed doors,
That open less but never more.

And when they start, go with the flow.
Excitement builds from head to toe.

Plaster crumbles, timbers fall,
Walls collapse in this great hall.

Letters jump at words, make phrases.
Meaning flies through empty mazes.

At last, you have a piece to share
With others willing, if you dare.

ALONE

It's not so bad to be alone.
To gaze at the stars, mind free to roam.
Not afraid to shine from within.
To love yourself is not a sin.

Quiet time is time well spent.
Not doing work or paying rent.
Select a topic, it's your choice
To sing out loud or with no voice.

Listen close to what you say
About your thoughts and feelings.
Do it once at least each day
To chart your course and dealings.

Be amazed at how you think
And what goes into your advice.
Don't decide without a blink
To act, instead think twice.

FLIGHT OF THE MONARCHS

There sits a gumdrop on a leave,
An egg of sorts, a short reprieve,
Before she breaks out of her shell,
Amazing story yet to tell.

Milkweed is her only feast.
There is no other best or least.
Two weeks from now, the change takes place.
Ordinary turns to lavender and lace.

Her splendor wrapped in untold strength.
Each year she flies the greatest length.
A path that leads to winter stay
On mountaintops where she will play.

Through winds that test the mightiest jets,
She soars through the skies without a rest.
Thousands of miles home she flies,
The pathway passed on when she dies.

Her mystery stored in ancient lore,
Two million years or maybe more.
A human guide provides no match
For such resolve these winds to catch.

What leads this wonder from her den,
To travel home, she's never been?
If only were the same for us,
To find that sacred place we trust.

NATIVE HERITAGE

Tell me to whom this land belongs:
To those who staked their claims and wronged
The natives living here who thrived
On nature, not what we contrived.
When birds rejoiced in trees abound,
Fresh air, clean water all around.

Those who took the better care
Deserve our founder's name to bear.
Their right to say what lies ahead:
A pathway full of hope instead
Of climate change, disease, and hate—
Respect for life, each other's fate.

How different is the claim they knew
From Ruthenians when they were slew
By barbarians living to the east,
Commissioned by an evil beast
To burn each city and each town,
Rape and kill and tear it down.

The natives' story nothing new;
The course we choose is what we do.
A change of heart, a major shift,
Not only right, a giver's gift.
Once told, the story comes to life,
Of peace and joy, an end to strife.

It's time for all who watched or took
To give it back much like the book.
The greatest story ever told
Means more than treasures full of gold.

To those we plundered, who have much less,
Apologize and give redress.

INEQUALITY

Stocks and bonds make millions grow
For many who will never know
Of those who wait for food in line,
While they eat their food and dine
In rooms adorned with lavish gold
Across from where the food stamps sold.

America the great, they say,
But not so true for those who pay
The price instead, cuz every day,
they face first-hand the life they dread,
a better choice than worse off dead.

Until such time that we can see
The curse of inequality,
We wake each day in our blind spot
And use the trinkets money bought
To forge ahead and cover our tracks
That lead right over others' backs.

Abuse of power leads one way.
While some pull up, most others will stay,
Until the gap so deep and wide
Becomes too big with nowhere to hide.
Take your dollar, change for dimes,
And feel the pleasure of giving ten times.

DIVE

Clear your mask and pull it down.
Fins are snug, shoes for a clown.
Down the beach like penguins stroll
Into the sea, your own fishbowl.
This, your favorite thing to do,
Alone or with the two of you.

Dive below and feel released
From worldly stress and come to peace
With ocean life that's all around,
A distant whale the only sound.
The coral shelf a masterpiece
With ancient memories released.

Just below the surface cruise
And take in sights before you lose
Another chance to see that fish,
So different from the menu dish.
Bright colors, beauty, so alive,
He looks you squarely in the eye.

The hours seem to melt away,
It's time to call another day.
I cry inside that I must go,
Tonight's tomorrow comes so slow.
Can't wait to see the next surprise,
I'll be here when the sun will rise.

CLOWN CONVENTION

A new day born by morning sun
Brings clowns to town with all their fun.

Our morning walk Auguste did spy
On unicycle riding by.

With spiked red hair and rounded nose,
Painted smile and baggy clothes.

We strolled along at a lively pace,
Greeting others with a smiling face.

We stopped for lunch around noontime;
There at the table sat a mime.

He looked to sip a cup of tea
Without the cup and pinkie free!

These antics sure to bring a grin
To all the young and those who've been.

From daily living time for pause,
To smile with others a noble cause.

The afternoon means time to meet,
To go inside and leave the street.

Imagine hundreds gathered round:
Hobos, tramps, all sorts abound.

Convening in that giant hall,
Clowns packed together wall to wall.

Some pulling rabbits from a hat,
While laughing, smiling where they sat.

The Emcee stepped upon the stage
To start his speech, read from the page.

He grabbed the mike and took his place,
A whipped cream pie smushed in his face!

The crowd of clowns hushed by the move,
A roar of laughter—they approved!

The Meeting now officially open.
Laughs came first, then words were spoken.

Awards will go to those who boast,
To make us smile and laugh the most.

DOG'S FIRST FLIGHT

Watching all those cars speed past,
I'd love to chase them, run so fast.
If only I could race about,
I'd chew that bumper, spit it out.

What's this place, so many humans,
Rolling bags, a shine-your-shoe man.
What's with this leash, goes round my chest?
She knows I like to run free best.
And what about the sign on me?
Emotional support? I need to pee.

Why did that man ask if I
Might need a muzzle or would try
To snap at those who pet and poke?
I ride on buses; I'm no dope.
I know when to clench my teeth
And when to open for a treat.

I've never walked through such a hall!
It's bigger than the lakeside mall
Where they clip my nails and hair.
Are those buses flying in the air?

This looks like number 49,
The bus we take all the time.
Wait, no, this bus is so darn big!
With seats so tight, what is this rig?

What's she doing in the aisle
With that life vest and a smile?
O good, we're on that ferry ride.

I like the park on the other side.
She's showing how to buckle in.
I'm glad I know how to swim.

Wait a minute, what's that roar?
She tightly fastened that big door.
I think we're moving on dry land.
Those engines whining, no one stands.
I wish the windows weren't so small,
I see sky, but no land at all!

STRAWBERRY MOON

Brilliant blue gives way to red.
Soon the sky turns pink instead.
Dusk arrives to turn the page,
As clouds give way to set the stage
For lunar pleasure, oh so sweet,
Like ripened berries at your feet.

In the east first signs appear,
A tiny sliver, then the sphere.
It lights the sky so large and bright.
A second chance at this day's light,
To mind the crops and tend the fields,
And pick sweet berries, eat the yield.

Ripened fruit that the pickers found
Leave lovely scents upon the ground.
It's Nature's way that once a year,
We see and smell these things so dear.
Soon the sun will rise again,
Casting shadows on the night that's been.

CLOUDS

Clouds like cotton candy float
In the sky above a boat
That sails to distant shores to find
Excitement of the newest kind.

Look up to see the tiger lies
together with a bird that flies
In search of fish for his next meal.
The sky, the sea, a circus feel.

Imagine life without TV.
The show begins if you can see
With open eyes as scenes unfold
The greatest stories ever told.

The sky so full, each cloud unique,
Some roar while others only peek.
A palette rich with blues and pink,
The contoured shapes your eyes help think.

The mountains rise and seem to grasp
At memories that mostly lapse.
It's time to savor more than ever
The times you share and love together.

SAILING

The plan was hatched when you awoke.
You packed your bags, no words were spoke.
The leaves were rustling at fifteen knots.
A perfect ten you both had thought.

From this window see the world.
A gleaming gem with sail unfurled,
About to hoist and cast away.
A lover's dream this breezy day.

Spread your wings, it's time to fly.
Crystal clear, a sunlit sky.
Azure blue the sea below.
Horizon beckons, brisk winds blow.

Rounded sail, the stays are taut.
The mainsheet fast by sailor's knot.
Enjoy the air we have all day
For dreaming, sharing, laughter, play.

HURRICANE

Curtains spread like angels' wings.
Gentle breeze helps chimes to sing.

Droplets dry on sweaty brow,
The calm before the storm is now.

Tomorrow brings our biggest test,
A gale and then a true tempest.

In such short time her tight embrace
Will shatter dreams to make her case.

The wind and rain cause so much pain.
When you act too slow, you act in vain.

What is lost what matters most,
Not those things with pride we boast.

Instead, we'll miss what we can't see,
Feeling we control our destiny.

The aftermath is still not clear,
As months go by, turn into years.

Instead, the writing's on the wall—
How we failed to heed the call.

THE BEACH

Pure white sand frames tides of time,
Like sunlit glass the seashells shine.
Strands of plastic, twisted weeds,
Bottle caps with fish line leads.
The day has come to clean the shore
Before it's gone forever more.

Old to young recount the story
Of when the beach was in its glory.
As we prospered and moved ahead,
We turned away from signs mis-read.
We should have acted with no debate,
To preserve our beaches' pristine state.

We cast our gaze toward better days,
Mesmerised by the soothing waves.
We made our beds with sheets so tight,
It choked what once was sand so bright.
Let's ban the plastic and clean the beach
To save the fish beyond its reach.

It's time to show we love the sea,
Caress the sand, get on our knees.
Watch footprints washed by waves that follow,
Children's laughter, not tears of sorrow.
When we can save nature's best,
What ensues is all the rest.

PLEASANT HILL

Outside the city, sun-splashed hills.
Cloud shaped shadows, valleys filled
With earth tone shades of greens and browns.
Bright blue skies spread all around.

Looking back the city gleams
In daylight, sparkles, built on dreams
Of those whose grit could make them real
By mixing gold with glass and steel.

The islands accent wind-swept waves,
As ferries crisscross through the bay.
An orange titan through the fog
Connects the hills with city smog.

A vibrance felt across this land,
As people cheer and take a stand.
For those from different lives they walk,
With common language they can talk.

CHAMPION

Determined to compete the best,
Greatest there ever was to see.
Exuberance with every test,
A champion so skilled as she.

A game much more than life to her,
The competition is the fun.
We watch amazed, her form a blur,
As rivals plummet one by one.

A time to shine and never fail,
Resilience on the lifetime trail.
To feel the low reveals the high
From deep below to reach the sky.

The will not just to do so well,
Instead to better than excel.
The one to watch with bated breath,
Her heart so big with moves so deft.

The court's a kingdom where she rules
With racquet as a magic rod.
Those who dare to join in duels,
Endure defeat on clay or sod.

FAMOUS

Today I'll travel in your shoes.
I know I have a lot to lose,
Because tomorrow I will be the same,
Only me without the fame.

So excited to finally feel
Adoration, admiration, mass appeal.
I'll bathe in all that limelight brings:
Excitement, energy, exotic things.

Oh, that's right, it also means
That people you don't know will scheme
To corner you, invade your space,
At every turn, in every place.

No longer any spot to hide,
To take a ride or walk outside.
Maybe I'll just change my mind,
Content to be the ordinary kind.

REFLECTION

The sun shines brightly in the eastern sky.
Your shadow is cast as the clothes start to dry.
What's now so clear was once hard to see.
The lessons we learned will shape what will be.

A gentle breeze caresses your cheeks
When you turn and gaze at the mountain peaks.
As the turtle dove stirs from her perch on the wall,
The sun casts shadows over all you recall.

The past highs and lows you can't see so clear,
But you lust for life at the same time you fear
That today is the finest of all the rest.
Trust that the future will bring what is best.

Distant waves sparkle like diamond rings,
Lost by lovers who find other things
To keep them happy each day as they play,
Longing for love so together they stay.

Look from behind to see what's ahead.
Do it each morning as you get out of bed.
Keep in your mind those thoughts that you like.
Those that you don't, feel happy to strike.

TRUTH

Why is it so hard to know
If what you say is black or white?
Or shades of grey, these seeds you sow.
Came straight from sources that you like.

How do you tell the good from bad,
The stories that are true from those that are fake?
Those that make you happy or make you sad,
Do they say what they mean for their own sake?

It's time to find your own way back,
To say what's right not just for you.
To redirect, then stay on track.
Don't be a parrot, speak what's true.

ALIVE

What does it mean to be alive?
To move ahead, to grow and thrive?
Take one minute of each day
To look at life in your own way.
To be aware of all that's good.
And all that's not, although it should.

What are your goals, the truths you dare
To speak that carry you from here to there?
What steps you take along the way
Will say to others how you play.
When life gets tough at every turn,
You look ahead with what you learn.

The morning sun ignites your day.
It doesn't matter, work or play.
Stretch and breathe to soak it in,
To realize how long it's been
Since you cherished life, remember when?

www.ingramcontent.com/pod-product-compliance
Lightning Source LLC
Chambersburg PA
CBHW060420050426
42449CB00009B/2049